Bees and Beekeepers

by Beth Lewis

Scott Foresman
is an imprint of

PEARSON

Glenview, Illinois • Boston, Massachusetts • Chandler, Arizona
Upper Saddle River, New Jersey

Photographs

Every effort has been made to secure permission and provide appropriate credit for photographic material. The publisher deeply regrets any omission and pledges to correct errors called to its attention in subsequent editions.

Unless otherwise acknowledged, all photographs are the property of Pearson Education, Inc.

Photo locators denoted as follows: Top (T), Center (C), Bottom (B), Left (L), Right (R), Background (Bkgd)

Cover Bettina Wehmeyer/Fotolia; **1** (T) Getty Images; **3** (C) DK Images; **4** (CL, C) Getty Images; **5** captblack76/Fotolia, (C) Knut Mueller/PhotoLibrary Group, Inc.; **6** Peter Anderson/©DK Images; **7** (C) Getty Images, (CL) Jupiter Images; **8** Bettina Wehmeyer/ Fotolia; **9** (C, BR) Getty Images; **10** (C) Getty Images, (BC) Jupiter Images.

ISBN 13: 978-0-328-50740-5
ISBN 10:   0-328-50740-7

9 10 11 12 V010 17 16 15 14 13

Many people don't like to be around bees. They are afraid they might get stung. But that's not true for a beekeeper. A beekeeper chooses to be around bees. Read on to find out more about a beekeeper's work!

Beekeepers use special hives that are made out of wood. Their hives are made of boxes that open at the top and bottom. Inside each box, the bees build their honeycombs on wooden frames that move.

A beekeeper's beehives

A beekeeper uses a tool called a smoker to spray smoke on the bees. The smoke helps keep the bees from stinging. This helps keep the beekeeper safe.

The beekeeper checks for eggs and young bees. He or she gives the bees sugar syrup if they need food. The beekeeper may also give them medicine.

Beekeepers wear special outfits that protect them from being stung.

Bees that live in a hive built by a beekeeper are like bees that live in the wild. Most of them are worker bees. These industrious, hard-working bees do many jobs. Some worker bees collect nectar and pollen from the flowers. Other worker bees store pollen, make honey, and clean the hive.

Bees live in a large group called a colony. A colony of bees lives in a hive.

There is one individual queen bee in each hive. She is the only bee that lays eggs. There are also drones. Drones do not work and cannot sting. They help the queen bee.

In late summer or fall, beekeepers take the frames from the hives to collect the honeycombs. Next, they put the honeycombs in a machine. The machine spins the honey and separates it from the comb. Then the combs are melted down to make wax.

A beekeeper with a frame

Some beekeepers sell honey and wax to factories. The factories then make goods with the honey and wax.

People use honey. Beeswax is made into candles, crayons, shoe polish, lipstick, and many other products. Many things we use every day start with bees and beekeepers!

Now Try This

Label the Parts

What parts of a beekeeper's outfit help him or her stay safe? What are these parts called? Look for the answers to these questions. Then draw a diagram of a beekeeping suit to show what you have learned.

1. Look in books, magazines, and on the Internet to find out about beekeeping suits.

2. Make a copy of a picture of a beekeeping outfit. You can use the one on page 5 of this book or another one that you find.

3. Use a dark marker to draw lines to each part of the outfit. Write the name of the part next to each line.

4. Share your diagram with the class.

Beekeeping
outfit